Getting Started: Foundation Rows

All beadwork projects begin with a foundation row, using either bugle beads or pairs of seed beads. Once you have completed the foundation row, you can proceed with any of the projects in this book.

Bugle Bead Foundation Row

Thread needle with two yards of thread, pulling one end of the thread to within three-fourths of the other.

1. Pass the needle through two bugle beads and slide them to within about six inches of the end of the long thread. This piece of thread will be worked into your completed project to finish it off. You may want to leave more or less than six inches depending on the type of project and your personal preference.

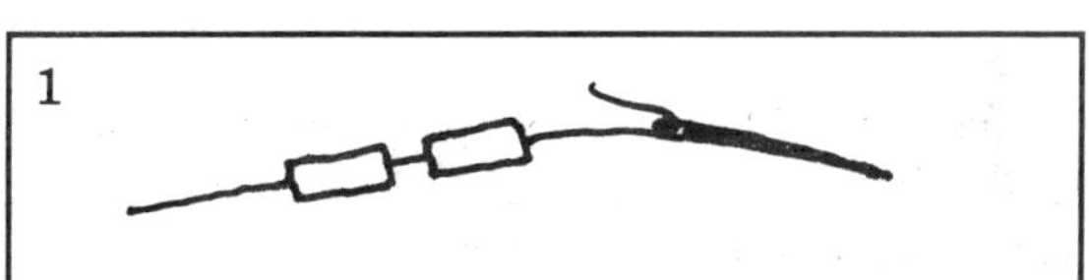

2. If you are right-handed, hold the first two bugle beads side by side, between the thumb and index finger of your left hand. The thread will be coming out the bottom of the second bead. Pass the needle back through the bottom of the first bugle bead. This will be referred to as passing the needle from the bottom to top of the bead throughout these instructions. Be sure to leave a tail at this time to be woven into your work later. If you are left-handed, you will hold the first two bugle beads side by side, between the thumb and index finger of the right hand. The thread will be coming out the bottom of the second bead. Pass the needle back through the bottom of the first bugle bead.

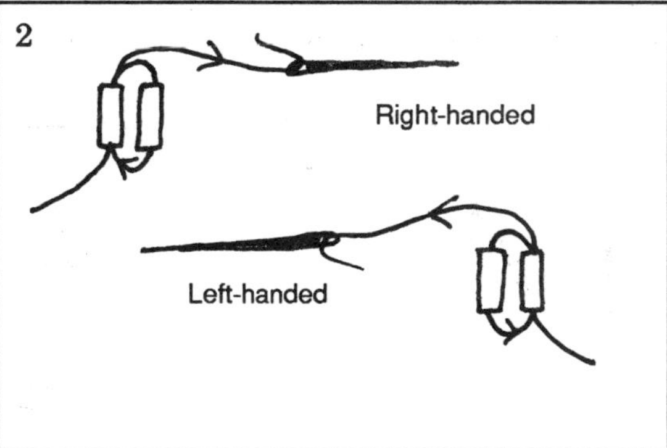

3. Now pass the needle through the second bugle bead again from the top to the bottom of the bead. With the beads between your thumb and index finger, hold the tail end of the thread so that it does not pull through. Now pull the thread with the needle so that the two beads are side by side and very snug. You are ready to add another bugle bead to the foundation. All beads in the foundation should be woven very snugly to give you a strong foundation and to give your work a neater look.

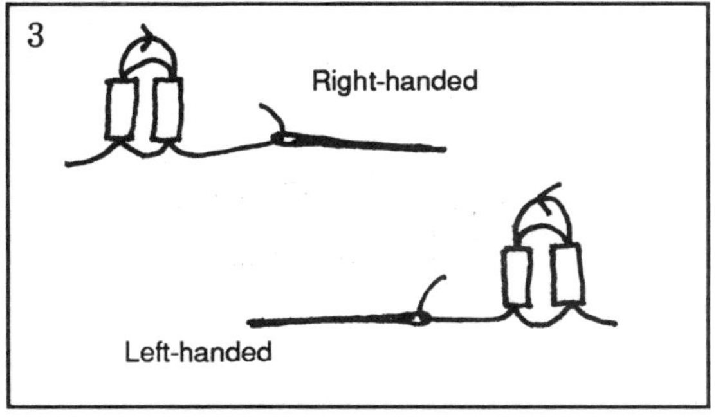

4. Pass the needle through the next bugle bead and slide it down the length of thread, placing it next to the second bugle bead. When the third bead is stood up against the second, the thread will be exiting from the top of the third bugle bead. Pass the needle back through the second bead from the top to the bottom. Then pass the needle through the third bugle from the bottom to the top. Be sure to pull the thread taut.

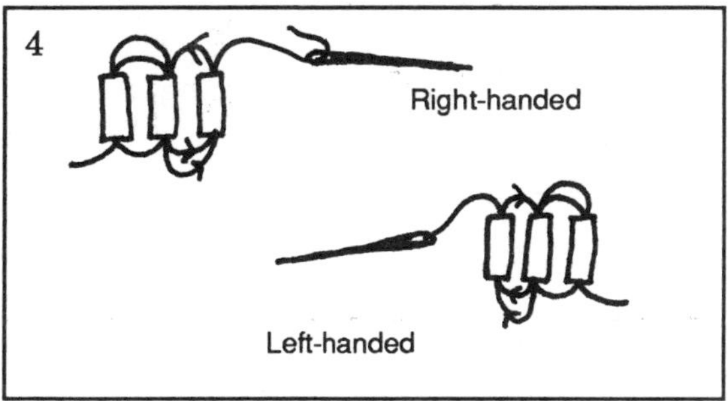

5. Continue adding beads in this manner until you have a foundation row of the desired number of bugle beads. When you add beads to your foundation, this will always be done in an alternating clockwise and counter-clockwise circular motion. Refer to the example below.

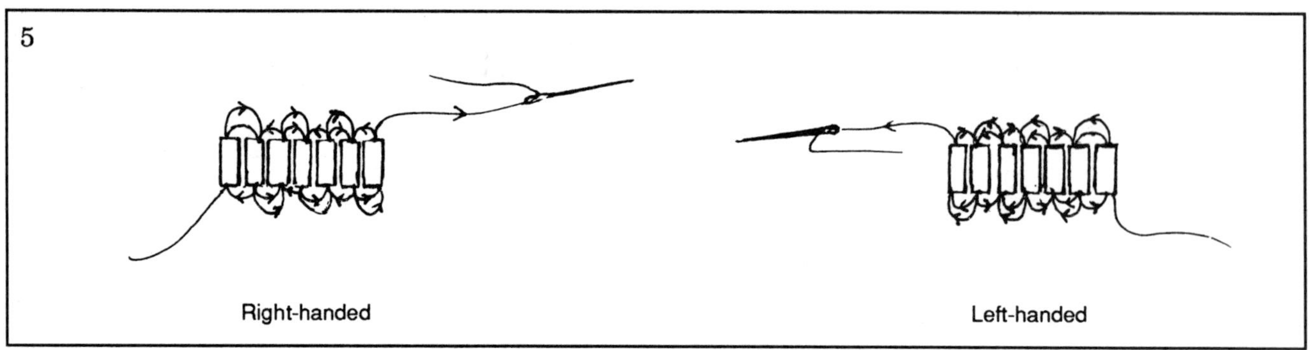

Seed Bead Foundation Row

Seed bead foundations are made in the same way as bugle bead foundations. The only difference is that you would string a pair of seed beads instead of one bugle bead. In other words, to begin the foundation row, you would string two pairs of seed beads. For the next step you would pass the needle through another pair of seed beads, bringing them side by side with the first set of seed beads. The diagrams below follow the same steps explained on the previous page in the bugle bead foundation row instructions. If referring back to instructions for bugle bead foundations, substitute two seed beads for each bugle bead.

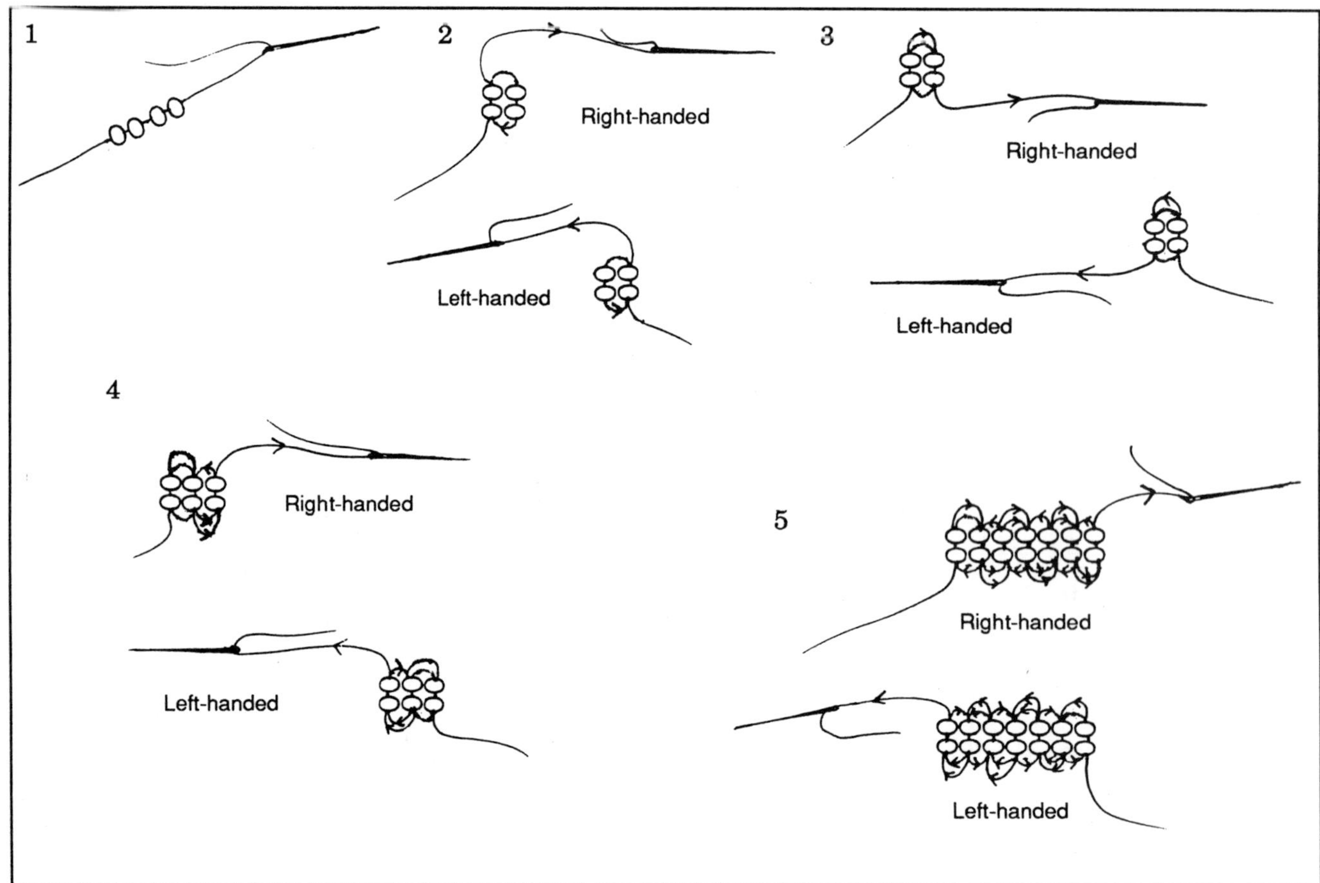

Creative Earrings and Barrettes

Each project pattern will specify the number of bugle beads or seed bead pairs in the foundation row. The * symbol marks the foundation row in each pattern. After the foundation row is completed, you are ready to start working on the remainder of the project. This section includes flat-style patterns for earrings and barrettes. I use either of two methods for these projects, depending on whether the project is made of single seed beads strung one at a time (Seed Bead Projects) or bugle beads (Bugle Bead Projects). Some of the projects use a "double woven" technique, in which rows of beads are added to both sides of the foundation row. This can be done using either seed or bugle beads.

SEED BEAD PROJECTS

If you are right-handed, hold the foundation row so that the thread with the needle is on the right side of the row. The thread should be coming out of the top of the last bead. If you are left-handed, hold the foundation row so that the needle is on the left side of the row.

Adding Additional Rows

1. Pick up one bead on the needle and slide it down the thread to the foundation. Going from the back side of the work to the front, pass the needle under the top thread which is connecting the first and second foundation row beads. Now pass the needle back through the bead you just added in the opposite direction the thread passed through the first time.

In other words, you are looping the thread around the top thread of the foundation row and fastening the bead in place by going through it in the opposite direction. Position the bead so that it is between the first and second pair of foundation row beads, and pull the thread snug. Pick up another bead on the needle and slide it down to the foundation row. You are ready for the next step.

2. The second bead is attached in the same manner as the first. You will pass the needle under the thread between the second and third pair of foundation row beads, and pass the needle back through the bead you just added. Pull the thread snug. Pick up another bead on the needle and slide it down to the foundation row. Continue adding beads to this row in this manner until you have added one bead between each foundation row pair.

3. When you are done, this row will have one less bead than the foundation row. If the foundation row has seven beads, this row will have six. When you finish this row, the thread with the needle will be on the left hand side of the work if you are right-handed and on the right side of the work if you are left-handed. Turn your work around so that the thread with the needle is toward the hand that will be using the needle.

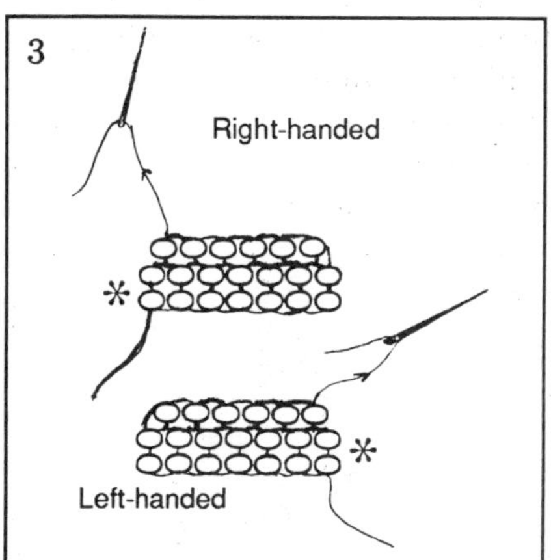

4. Start the next row just like you did the previous one. Pick up a bead and slide it down the thread. Pass the needle under the thread that connects the first and second beads of the second row. Pass the needle back through the bottom of the bead just added and pull the thread snug. The needle should always be passed under the thread

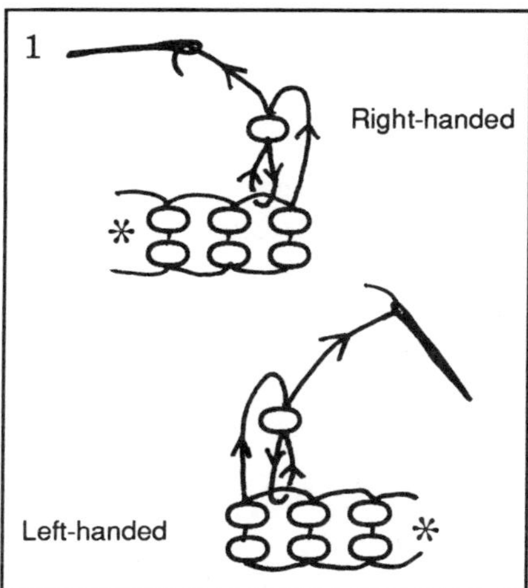

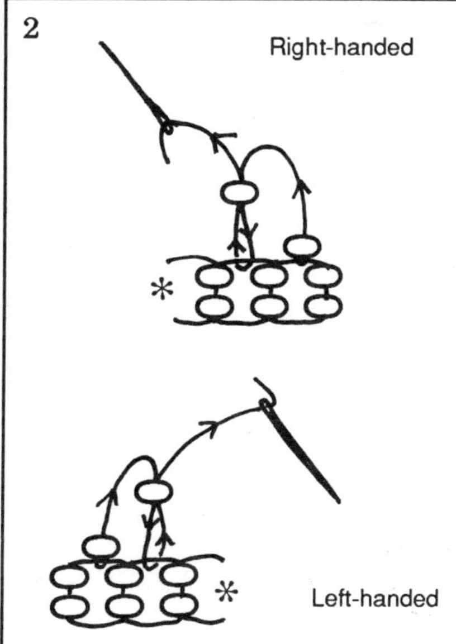

from the back side of the work toward you. When you complete this row it will have one less bead than the previous row.

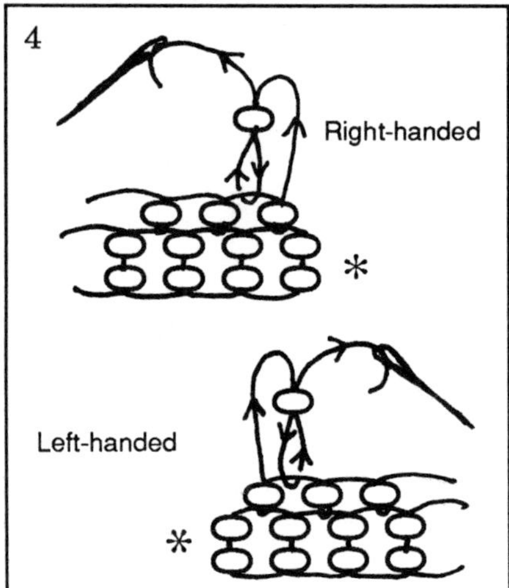

5. For earring projects, continue adding rows until you end up with a row of only two seed beads. The last bead you add in this row is bead #1 in the illustration. You are now ready to add the loop at the top of the earring so that the earwire can be attached. Pick up four or six seed beads on the needle, depending on how wide you want the loop, and slide them down the thread. Pass the needle through bead #2 from the top to the bottom. Pull the thread snug. To give the loop more strength, pass the needle back through bead #1 from the bottom to the top.

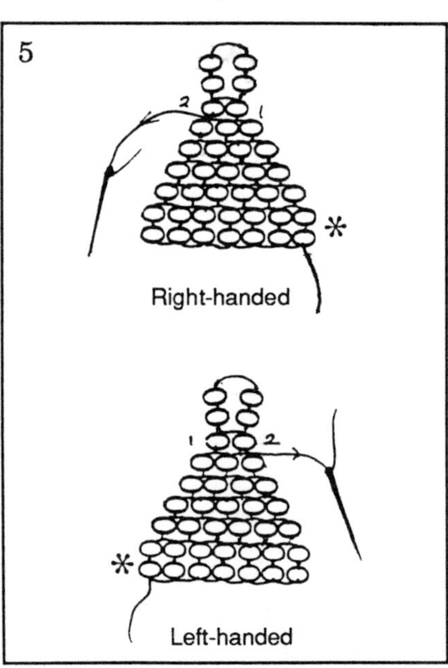

6. Go through the four or six beads of the hanging loop, and then go through bead #2 again from the top to the bottom.

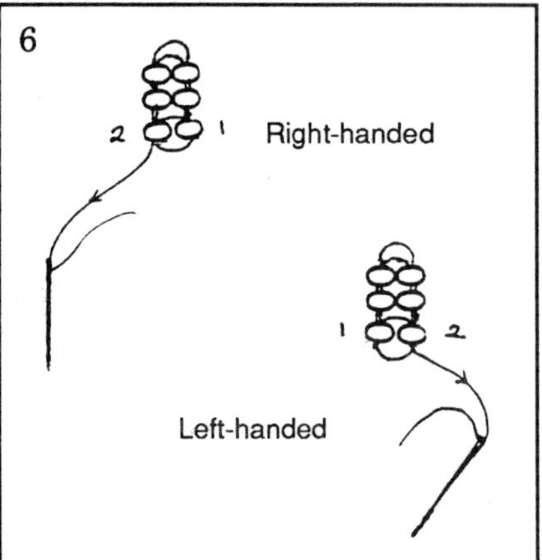

Attaching the Fringe

7. You are now ready to finish off the earring by attaching fringe to the bottom. You need to bring the needle and thread back to the foundation row so that the fringe can be added. To do this, pass the needle through the beads along one side of the earring, from top to bottom.

Pass the needle through the last pair of foundation row beads (or if bugle bead foundation, the last bugle bead) so that the thread is exiting the foundation row from the bottom of the work.

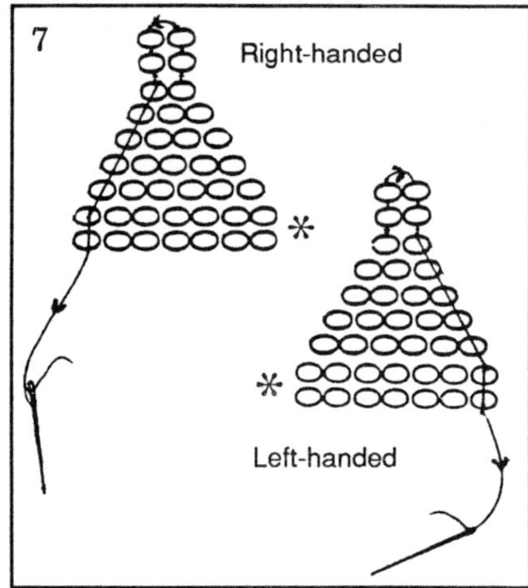

8. Thread the needle through the desired number of seed and bugle beads to make the first fringe. Pass the needle once through the end bead or beads (usually the fringe will end with either one or three

beads). Then pass the needle back through the beads of the fringe from the bottom to the top and back through the beads of the foundation row. In the example below, the needle is passed through the fringe beads twice, with the exception of the three beads at the bottom. The thread is passed through these three beads only once. If you are using a single bead at the end of the fringe, you will pass the needle back through all the beads of the fringe twice, except for the last bead added, which will be passed through only once.

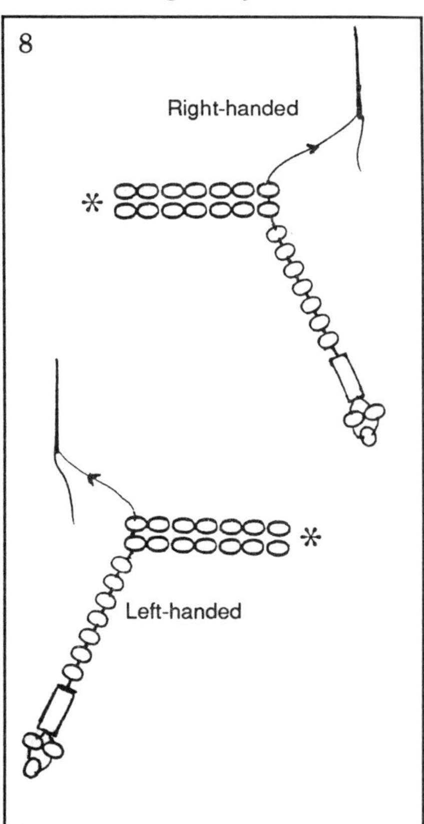

Finishing

9. To finish the earring, weave the needle and thread from bottom to top through the beads along the side of the earring to which the last fringe is attached. This will be just the reverse of what you did in step 7. Go through the beads of the loop for the ear wire and weave through a couple of beads at the top of the work. Clip the thread close to the bead where you wish to end. This thread is finished off. To finish off the tail you left at the start of the instructions, you will need to thread the tail through the eye of the needle and weave the thread through the foundation row. Clip the thread close to the bead where you wish to finish and the earring is complete. Weaving the threads back into the work gives the finished project a neater look than tying knots. If you want, you can use a little bit of clear fingernail polish to secure the thread where you are ending the work. This is optional. Be sure not to get a lot of clear nail polish on your finished project as it will make your beadwork stiff and could change the color of some of the beads.

Rose Hair Barrette
(Project B)

This project was made using size 11 seed beads and size 5 bugle beads. For this project, you will need:

- 330 opaque white seed beads
- 17 light pink seed beads
- 15 light green seed beads
- 16 dark green seed beads
- 79 metallic gold seed beads
- 327 silver lined red seed beads
- 64 opaque black bugles
- a piece of black felt 2 inches by 4 inches
- white and black size D beading thread
- a french hair clip 3 inches long
- two rose appliqués

Do the bead work just as you would a pair of earrings, following the graph and using white beading thread. The foundation row is 31 beads long. When you have finished the bead work, cover the french hair clip with black felt. Sew the finished bead work to the hair clip, using the black beading thread. Center the roses, one on each end of the clip. Set the roses in place with craft glue.

Turquoise Teardrops
(Project H)

This project was made using size 11 seed beads and size 5 bugle beads. This pattern uses a foundation row of 11 pairs of seed beads. To make this pair of earrings, you will need:

- 42 metallic turquoise seed beads
- 67 metallic silver seed beads
- 162 opaque black seed beads
- 11 opaque black bugle beads

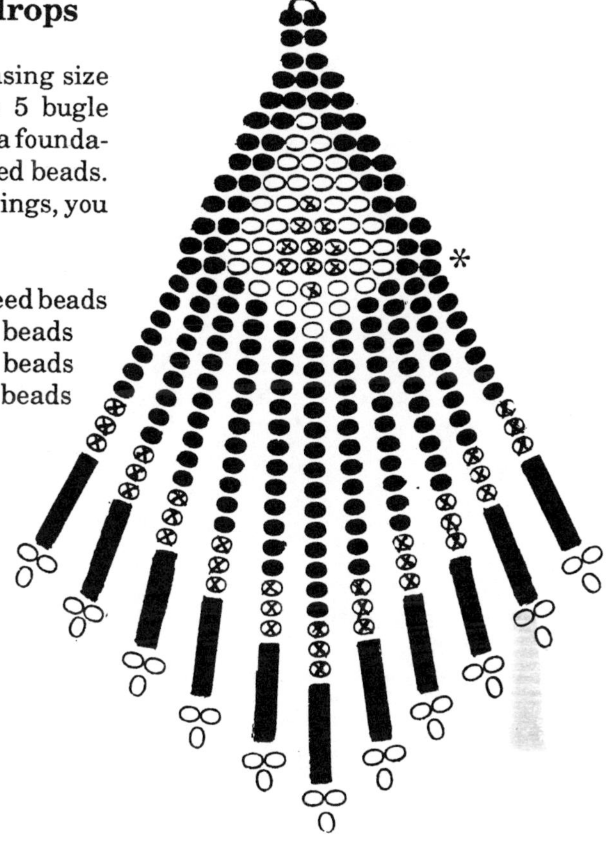

○ Silver washed
⊗ Metallic turquoise
● Black

▌ Black bugle

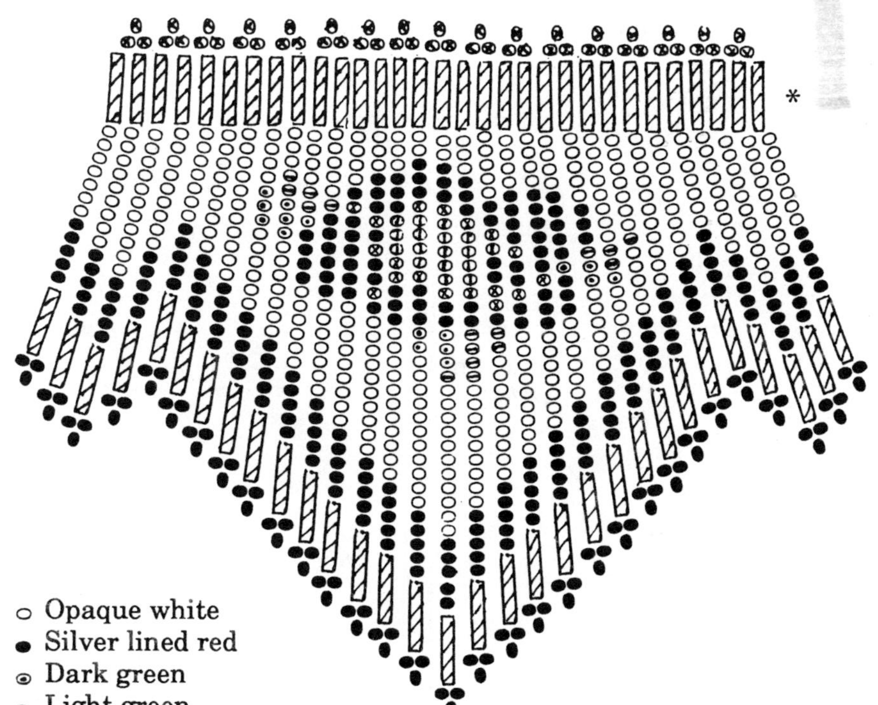

○ Opaque white
● Silver lined red
⊘ Dark green
⊕ Light green
⊗ Metallic gold
⊕ Light pink

▨ Black bugle

* Foundation row

BUGLE BEAD PROJECTS

(NOTE: This method can also be used for projects in which seed beads are added to a row as a unit pair, or whenever you do not want any threads to show on the finished project.)

1. Pick up two bugle beads on the needle and slide them down to the foundation row. Pass the needle under the top thread that connects the second and third beads of the foundation row. Now pass the needle from top to bottom back through the second of the two bugle beads you just added. Position this bead between the second and third beads of the foundation row and pull the thread snug.

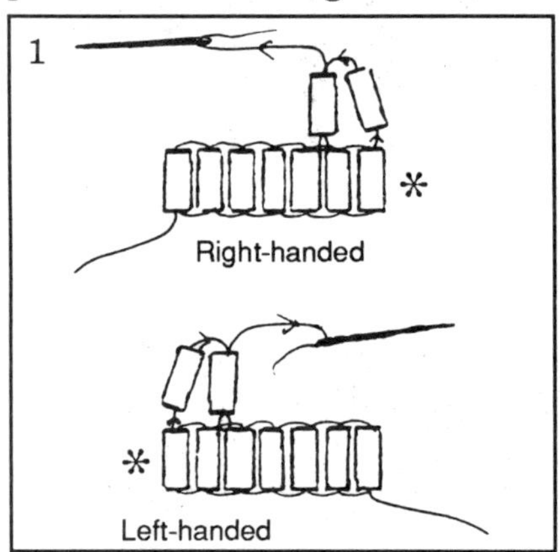

2. After adding the first two bugle beads, all other beads in this new row are added one at a time. Pick up a bugle bead on the needle and slide it down to your work. Pass the needle under the thread that

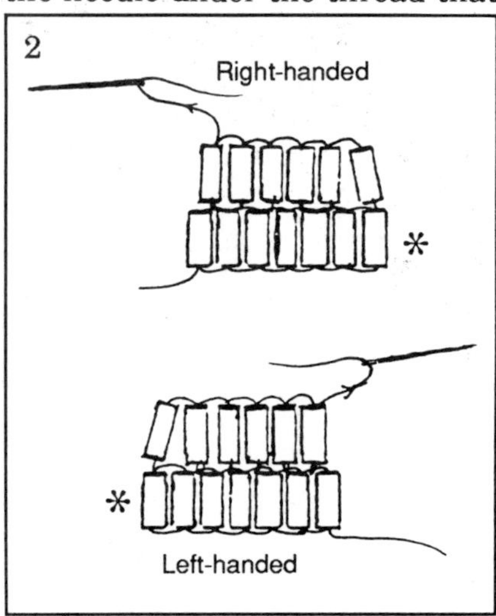

connects the third and fourth beads of the foundation row. Then pass the needle back through the bottom of the bugle bead that you just added. Refer to illustration 2. Continue adding beads in this manner to complete this row. You will have one less bead in this new row than you have in the foundation row. Turn the work around so that the thread with the needle is exiting toward the hand that holds the needle.

3. You are ready to start the next row. Pick up two bugle beads on the needle and slide them down as you did in step one of these instructions. Pass the needle under the thread that connects the second and third bugle beads of the previous row. Now pass the needle back through the bottom of the second bugle bead only.

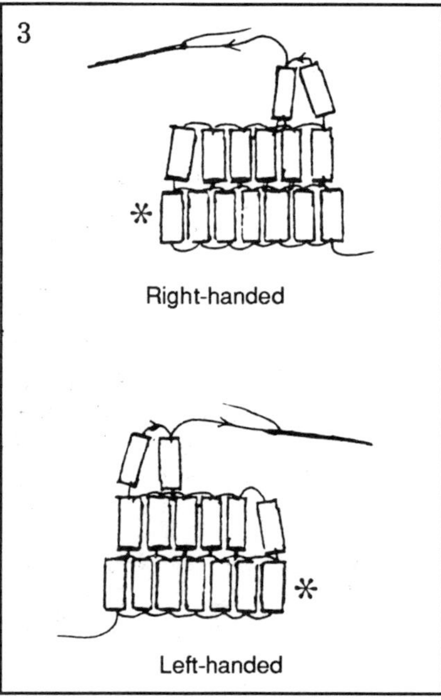

Pull the thread snug and position the bead so that it is between the second and third bugle beads of the previous row. Continue adding rows in this manner until you complete a row of only two bugle beads. Attach the ear wire loop as in step 5 on page 4. The loop should always be made with seed beads.

Adding Fringe

4. Using this method, the first bead of each row will be slightly out of position at this point. Since you need to bring the needle back to the foundation row to add the fringe, you can bring these beads into position at the same time you weave the needle back to the foundation row. Follow the direction of the arrows and weave the needle through the beads as shown in the illustration. Pull the thread snug as you do this. Finish adding fringe to the bottom of the project in the manner explained in steps 7 and 8 on page 4.

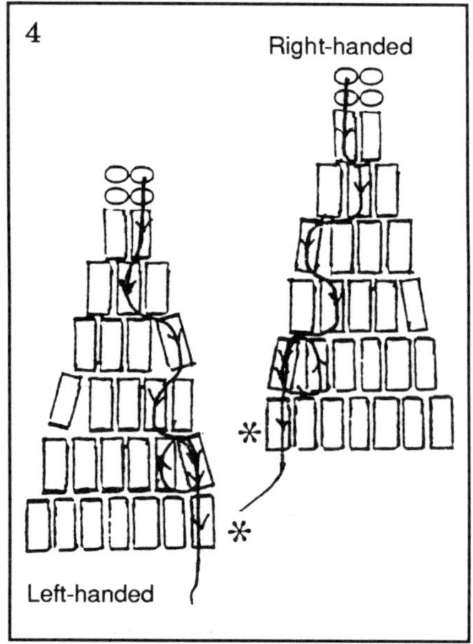

Finishing

5. You can now finish off the project and bring the beads on the other side in line at the same time. The needle will be woven through the first and second bugle beads of the rows the same way as it was done to bring the needle to the foundation row. The only difference will be that you will go from the foundation row to the top of the project or earring. Weave the needle and thread through the beads indicated in the examples, opposite, in the same direction as the arrows. Weave the tail through the foundation row and secure the thread as explained in step 9 on page 5. This project is completed.

Interlocking Blues
(Project A)

This pair of earrings was made using size 2 bugle beads and size 11 seed beads. The foundation row consists of 9 bugle beads. To make this pair of earrings you will need:

- a pair of silver ear wires
- 66 dark blue bugle beads
- 66 light blue bugle beads
- 24 silver bugle beads
- 228 silver seed beads

Lavender and Silver
(Project N)

This pair of earrings was made using size 2 bugle beads and size 11 seed beads. The foundation row consists of 9 bugle beads. To make this pair of earrings you will need:

- a pair of silver ear wires
- 52 silver bugle beads
- 86 lavender bugle beads
- 134 silver seed beads
- 54 lavender seed beads

You could make a matching necklace by making a third earring and attaching it to a silver chain using a small jump ring.

* Foundation row

Deco Diamonds
(Project I)

This pair of earrings was made using size 2 bugle beads and size 11 seed beads. The foundation row consists of 9 bugle beads. For this pair of earrings you will need:

- 39 silver bugle beads
- 30 opaque black bugle beads
- 90 opaque black seed beads

▢ Silver bugle

▮ Black bugle

● Black

* Foundation row

Double Woven Method

A double woven earring is started in the same manner as the methods just described up to the point of adding the fringe. This technique can be used for either seed bead or bugle bead projects.

1. When you have completed the top part of the project or earring and have brought the needle and thread back to the foundation row, instead of adding fringe you weave the other half of the design, following the graph, in the same manner as for the top of the earring. When you bring the needle back to the foundation row, turn the work upside down. This puts the foundation row up, making it easier to start beading the other half of the design. Follow the basic instructions and add the necessary rows to complete the pattern. Instead of ending with a loop for the ear wire, you will continue adding rows until you add a row of only one bead, if you are making a diamond-shaped pattern.

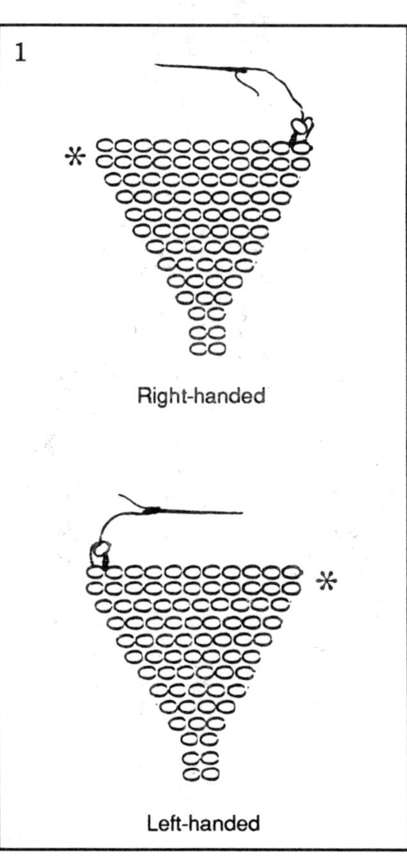

2. After adding the final bead, weave the needle back to the foundation row as indicated in the illustration. Turn the earring right side up or with the ear wire loop at the top of the earring. You will add fringe a little bit differently when you use this technique. Weave the needle through one side of the beadwork so that it exits from the bottom of the desired bead, and add the desired fringe beads. Pass the needle back through the same bead you started from and weave the needle to the adjacent bead to add the next fringe. After you have completed adding all the fringes, finish off the project as explained in step 9 on page 5.

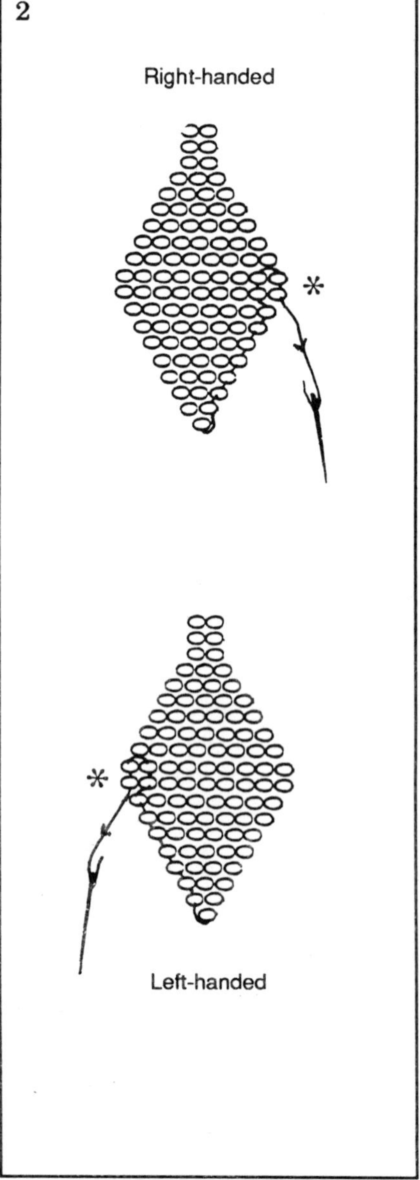

Japanese Lanterns
(Project F)

The foundation row for this pair of earrings consists of 9 bugle beads. All seed beads are size 11; bugle beads are size 3. To make this pair of earrings, you will need:

- 10 25-mm lavender bugle beads
- 38 lavender bugle beads
- 106 white seed beads
- 90 metallic pink seed beads
- 10 burgundy seed beads
- a pair of ear wires

○ White
◉ Burgundy
⬮ Metallic pink

▮ Lavender #3 bugle

▮ Lavender 25-mm bugle

Festive Barrettes
(Projects G and M)

These hair barrettes are made using the double woven method. After completing the foundation row, add two rows to the top and two rows to the bottom of the foundation row.

Because the beadwork for these barrettes will not be sliding around on the hair clip, these projects work well using the metallic washed colors. Also, because the beadwork is small and has less weight than a barrette with fringe, you may use a good craft glue or cement to fasten the bead work in place. I have never had a problem with slippage using this technique.

After the beadwork is completed for the barrette, weave the needle and thread through the last row of the beadwork on the top and bottom. This will give your work some added strength. After you have glued the beaded piece to the hair clip and the glue has dried completely, you may want to apply a light coat of clear fingernail polish to the beaded piece. This will help to protect the beads' metallic wash and keep them looking nicer longer.

The foundation rows for each of the 2 3/8-inch french hair barrettes projects have 29 pairs of size 11 seed beads. For the 2-inch barrettes, the foundation rows have 24 pairs of size 11 seed beads.

As you'll notice, project M2 has two patterns included. The first is for the project pictured on the cover. The second pattern is not pictured on the cover. I hope this will encourage you to experiment with patterns and colors on your own. You really cannot go wrong with these metallic washed colors. Go ahead—be daring!

Four Diamonds
(Project K)

The foundation row for this pair of earrings consists of 9 pairs of seed beads. All seed beads are size 11; bugle beads are size 2. To make this pair of earrings, you will need:
- 210 gun metal grey seed beads
- 18 small black glass beads
- 102 white seed beads
- 154 grey seed beads
- 36 black bugle beads
- a pair of ear wires

▮ Black bugle

◆ Small black glass bead

○ White
◉ Grey
⊕ Gun metal grey

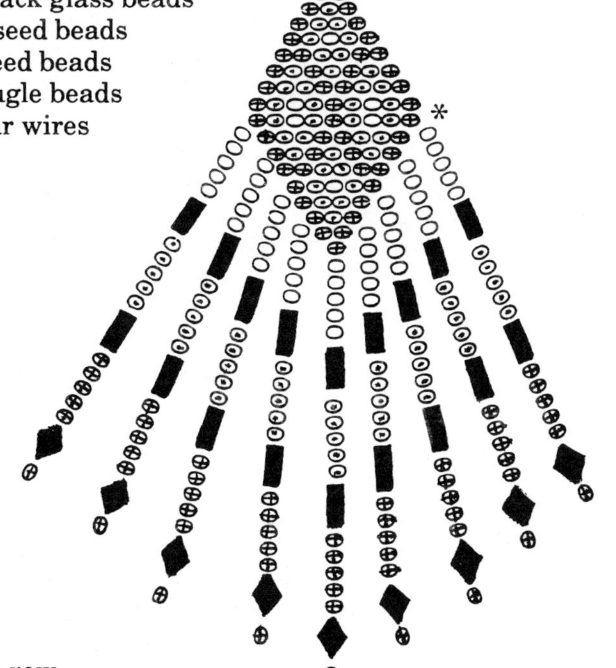

* Foundation row

Festive Barrette Patterns

Project G1
2 3/8-inch french hair clip
◯ Metallic gold (48)
⊕ Metallic turquoise (10)
⬤ Carnival color (110)

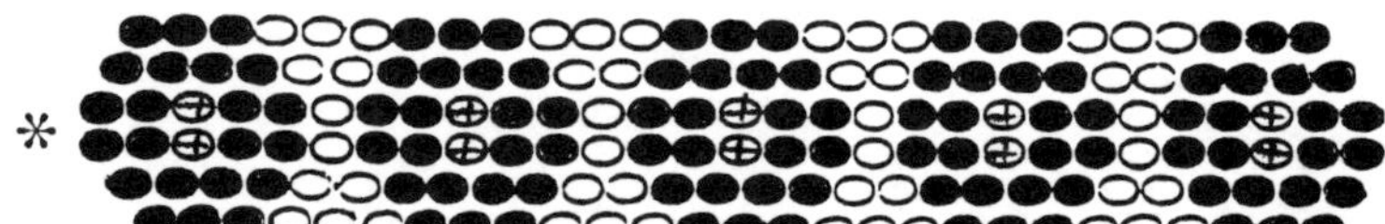

Project G2
2 3/8-inch french hair clip
◯ Metallic silver (26)
⊕ Metallic dark purple (24)
☉ Metallic light purple (24)
⊖ Metallic dark pink (24)
⬤ Metallic light pink (24)
⊕ Metallic turquoise (24)
⬤ Metallic light green (22)

Project G3
2-inch french hair clip
⊕ Dark green (46)
◯ Light green (16)
⬤ Metallic light green (76)

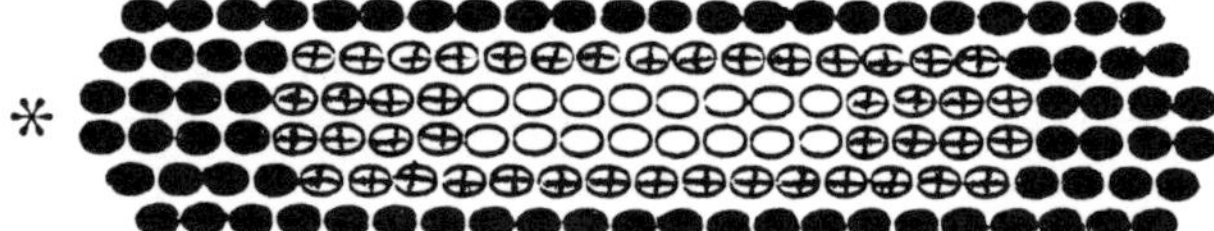

Project G4
2-inch french hair clip
◯ Metallic silver (78)
⊜ Metallic turquoise (30)
⬤ Metallic dark pink (30)

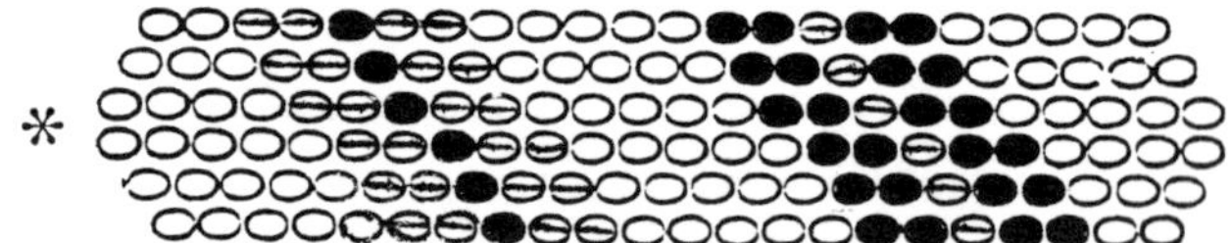

Project M1
2-inch french hair clip
◯ Dark grey (66)
⬤ Metallic light grey (72)

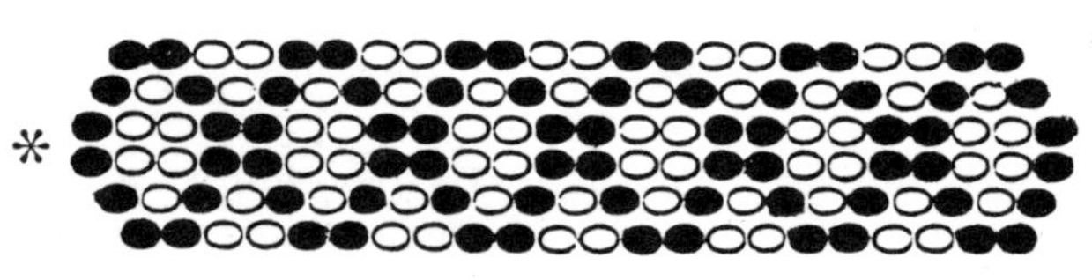

Project M2
2 3/8-inch french hair clip
◯ Metallic silver (96)
⊕ Metallic dark pink (36)
⬤ Metallic turquoise (36)

Project M3
2 3/8-inch french hair clip
◯ Light lavender (85)
⬤ Metallic dark purple (83)

Project M4
2-inch french hair clip
◯ Metallic silver (98)
⊕ Metallic turquoise (8)
⬤ Carnival color (32)

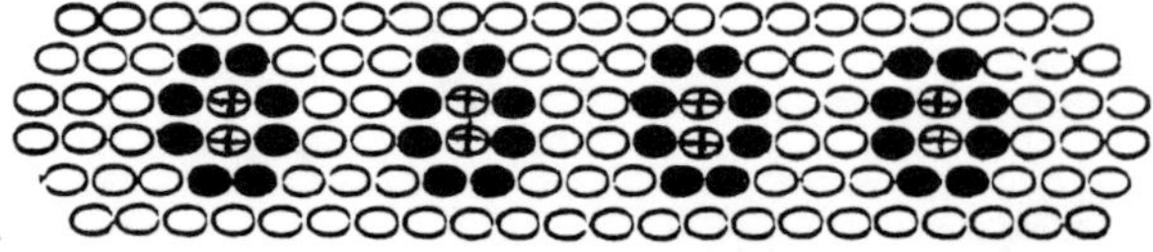

* Foundation row

Cylindrical Projects

You can use this method to make lighter covers and tubular projects such as earrings and necklaces. It is not necessary to use a loom with this technique. This type of beading lends itself very well to diamond designs but can be adapted for flowers or other types of designs. This method works well for covering cylindrical shapes that are uniform in circumference from top to bottom. For example, it is easy to make covers for Bic lighters because they have smooth sides and are the same size at the bottom as they are at the top.

The earrings and necklace described in this section were made using 1/4 inch or 3/32 inch K & S Tubing, which can be purchased at your local hobby shop. I use K & S Brass Tubing because it is harder than copper tubing and the walls are thinner. Your finished project will be close to the size of the tubing used.

Lighter Covers

1. Begin with a piece of beading thread about two to three yards long. To start a lighter cover, you will make a foundation row of 30 pairs of seed beads (size 11). Once you complete the foundation row, without twisting it, join the two ends together. Weave the needle through several beads of the foundation row on both sides of where it is joined. This prevents the foundation row from gapping once you start the next row. Your foundation row is now a circle. Insert the lighter through the middle. Slide the foundation row toward the flint end of the lighter. This will be referred to as the top.

2. The instructions for this step will be the same for either hand, so only one diagram is given.

Once you have slid the foundation row onto the lighter, be sure to pull the threads so that the work will be as snug as possible. The foundation row will be a little loose at this point, but it will become tighter once you add the next row.

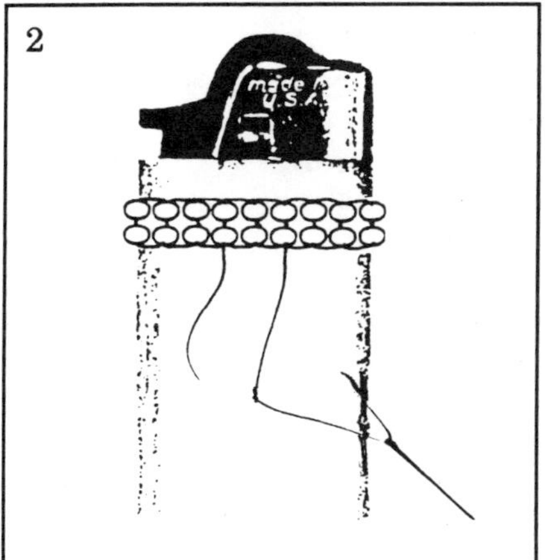

3. Bic lighters are an oval shape, so you will want to hold the lighter so that the flat side is facing you and the curved side is facing the hand that holds the needle. Beads in this row will be added in the same manner that they are added in the basic instructions (see steps 1 and 2 on page 3). It will be easier to slide the needle under the thread if you add beads to each row where the lighter is curved. You will want to slide the foundation row to the right if you are right-handed or to the left if you are left-handed.

Pick up a bead on the needle and slide it to the foundation row. This bead will be positioned between the first and second pairs of foundation row beads. Pass the needle between the pairs of foundation row beads, under the thread that connects them. Bring the needle toward you and pull the bead you are adding to the foundation row, centering it in the first space. Now pass the needle back through the bead you are adding, from top to bottom. Move the foundation row about the space of one bead to the left if you are right-handed, and to the right if you are left-handed. You are ready to start the next row.

4. Pick up a bead with the needle. Pass the needle under the thread that connects the second and third pair of foundation row beads. Now pass the needle back through the bead you are adding to the row, from top to bottom. Pull the thread so that the two beads of this row are side by side and centered over the spaces of the foundation row. Continue adding beads to this row by moving the lighter cover around the lighter about the space of one bead every time.

When you complete the new row, you will have the same number of beads in this row as you did in the foundation row. For example, if you start your project with a foundation row of 30 pairs of seed beads,

then every row in the project will have 30 beads. When you come to the area where the tail is, move it out of the way by pulling it up over the foundation row to the top of the lighter. You will work the tail into the finished work when the project is complete.

5. To close this row, take the needle up through the first bead added to the row, from bottom to top, and then down through the second bead added. Pull the thread snug and adjust the beads in the row so that they are centered between the foundation row beads.

You are ready to start the next row. Continue adding rows to the lighter cover following steps 3 and 4 of these instructions throughout the project, until you need to add more thread. If you begin with a length of thread about two yards

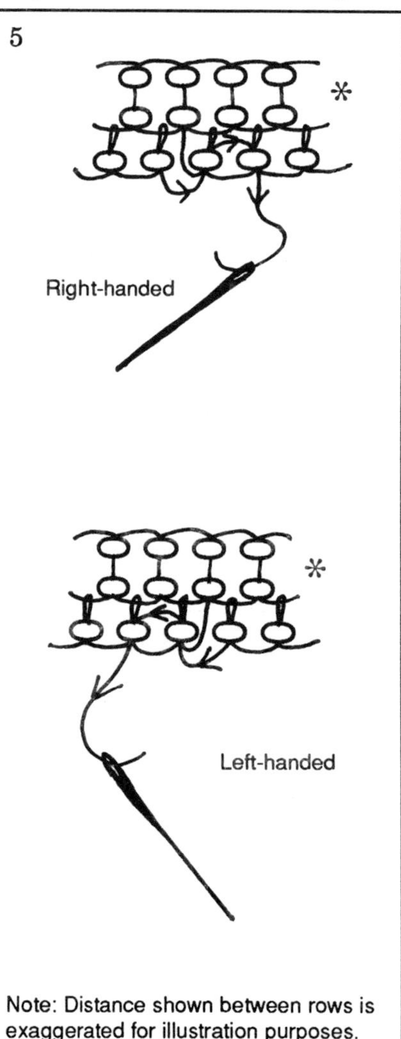

Note: Distance shown between rows is exaggerated for illustration purposes.

long, you will have to add thread more often throughout the project than if you start with three yards. If you begin with three yards, you will not have to add thread as often; however, it will be harder to use at first as it has a tendency to snarl and twist. It's up to you how much thread you start with.

6. When you need to add thread, first complete the row you are working on. Weave through three or four of the first beads in the row you just completed as you would when you are closing a row and slip the needle off the thread, leaving about a 10-inch tail. Insert another two- or three-yard section of thread onto the needle.

Skip about three or four beads from where you ended the other thread and pass the needle up through one bead of the bottom row and down through the next bead, just as you did to the end of the last row.

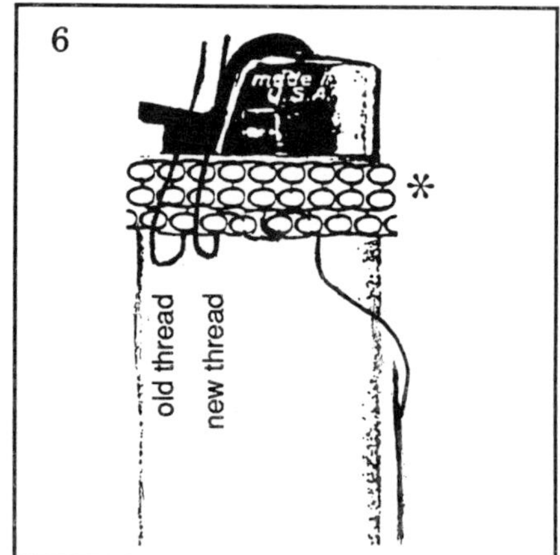

Repeat this for about four more beads and bring the needle and thread to the bottom of the work so that you can start the next row. Start the next row as you would any other row. When you come to the end of this row, you will run into the thread tails left dangling from the end of the previous row and the start of the current row.

Move these threads out of the way by bringing them up over the top of the rows you have completed and continue to add beads until the row is closed. Be careful not to catch these threads with the needle. Doing so could bring them into your work. Continue adding rows to the lighter cover until you are ready to add another thread. Then finish off the thread as instructed earlier by going back to the end of the thread and weaving it through about five or six rows of beads. Slide the work off the lighter and pass the needle through a bead toward the inside of the work. Clip the thread very close to the bead and that piece is finished off. Repeat this for the tail of thread. Add another piece of thread and you are ready to continue on.

When you have completed the last row of the lighter cover, weave the needle back and forth through the last row all the way around. Clip the thread very close to the bead where the thread exits and apply a little bit of clear fingernail polish if desired. Go back to the tail of the foundation row and weave it into the foundation row as you did the last row of the project. Clip and apply a small amount of clear fingernail polish here, also, if desired. Do not use fingernail polish to finish off any threads except the foundation thread and the end of the last row of the project.

7. To use the graph for projects using this method, you will need to imagine that the graph is what the finished project would look like if it were clipped apart and laid flat. You will add beads according to the graph to make a design just as you would to make a pair of earrings; the only difference is that you are forming a cylinder. So when you complete a row and start another, find the bead on the graph from which the thread is exiting.

Go to the next row. The bead on the graph that is exactly centered between the bead your thread exits from and the next bead to the right (or to the left if you are left-handed) is the bead you will add first to start the next row. In the final row, the beads are added as unit pairs for a nicer finish.

Crown and Jewels
(Project L)

To make this lighter cover you will need:

- 80 silver seed beads
- 170 blue seed beads
- 220 red seed beads
- 115 black seed beads
- 265 white seed beads

This lighter cover is made using size 10 seed beads, so there will be fewer rows and fewer beads in each row compared to the lighter covers on the following page. The foundation row has 25 pairs of seed beads.

- ○ Opaque white
- ● Opaque black
- ⊙ Silver lined blue
- ⊖ Silver lined red
- ⏀ Silver

* Foundation row

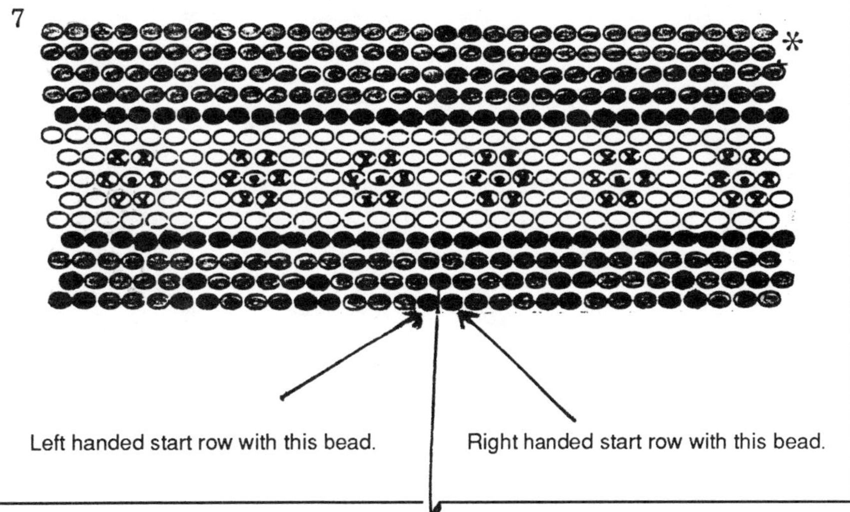

Misty Harbor
(Project C)

This lighter cover was made using size 11 seed beads. The foundation row has 30 pairs of seed beads. To make this lighter cover, you will need:

- 552 dark blue seed beads
- 174 pink seed beads
- 360 white seed beads
- 84 fuschia seed beads
- 180 medium blue seed beads

   ○ Dark blue
   ⊖ Medium blue
   ● White
   ⊛ Fuschia
   ⊕ Pink

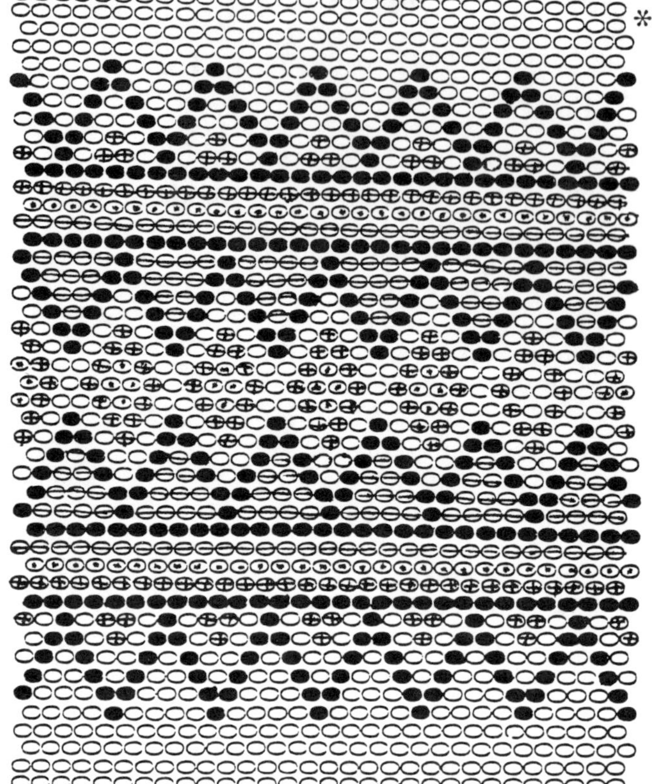

Indian Blanket
(Project D)

This lighter cover was made using size 11 seed beads. The foundation row has 30 pairs of seed beads. To make this lighter cover, you will need:

- 444 gun metal seed beads
- 354 opaque white seed beads
- 240 opaque grey seed beads
- 312 silver-lined red seed beads

   ○ White
   ⊖ Grey
   ⊙ Red
   ● Gun metal

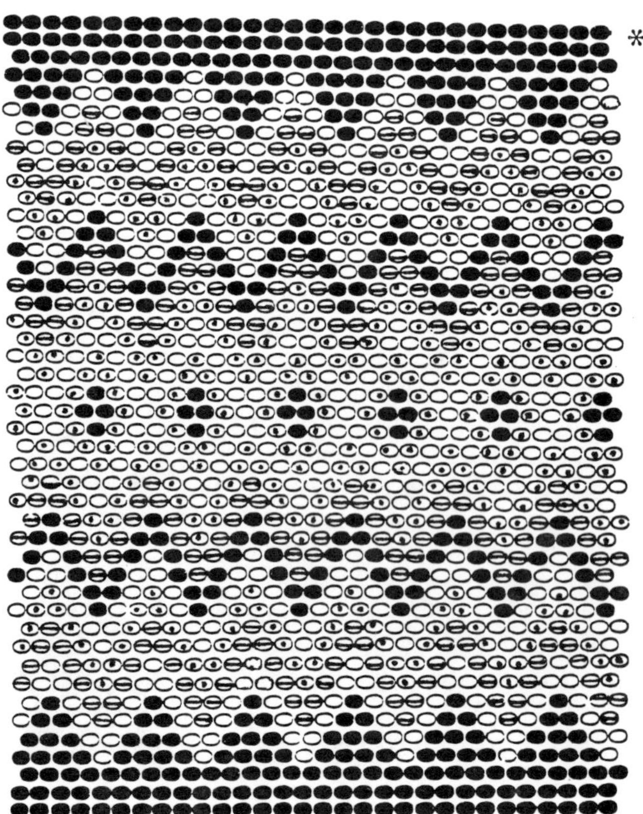

* Foundation row

Springtime Flowers
(Project O)

This lighter cover was made using size 11 seed beads. The foundation row has 30 pairs of seed beads. To make this lighter cover, you will need:

- 420 light blue seed beads
- 342 dark blue seed beads
- 432 white seed beads
- 120 light pink seed beads
- 12 burgundy seed beads
- 24 light green seed beads

⊖	Light blue
●	Dark blue
○	White
⊕	Light pink
⊙	Burgundy
⊕	Light green

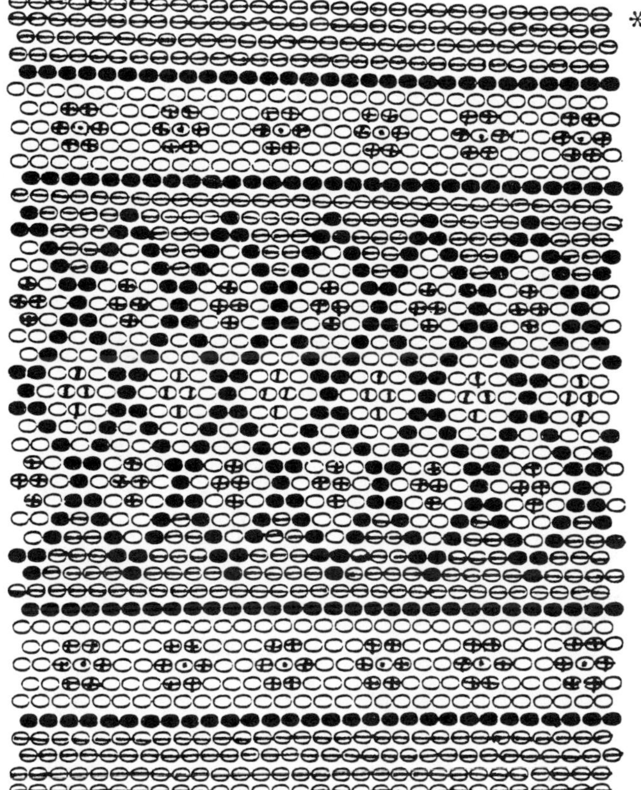

Repeating Diamonds
(Project P)

This lighter cover was made using size 11 seed beads. The foundation row has 30 pairs of seed beads. To make this lighter cover, you will need:

- 678 opaque white seed beads
- 168 light green seed beads
- 504 dark green seed beads

○	White
⊙	Light green
●	Dark green

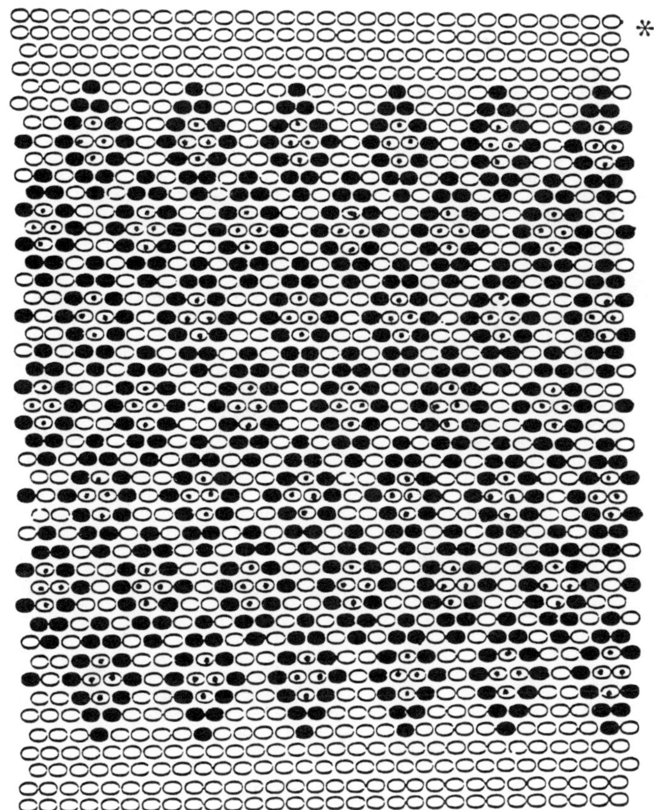

* Foundation row

Burgundy Elegance
(Project E)

This project was made using size 11 seed beads and various sizes of glass beads, described below. The foundation row has 12 pairs of seed beads. To make this necklace you will need:

- 1/4-inch piece of brass tubing, approximately six inches long
- 912 burgundy seed beads
- 760 metallic pink seed beads
- 384 light pink seed beads
- 24 8-mm faceted glass beads
- 16 8-mm burgundy faceted glass beads
- 6 8-mm diamond shaped glass beads
- 1 10-mm diamond-shaped glass bead
- one silver necklace clasp
- size F beading thread to string the necklace together

Make eight tubular shapes on a piece of brass tubing 1/4-inch in diameter, following the graph. Finish off each tubular shape after completion. Using size F thread, string the necklace together following the illustration at right.

⬤ Silver lined burgundy
◯ Light pink
◒ Metallic pink

⬤ Burgundy 8-mm glass bead

◯ Crystal 8-mm glass bead

◇ Crystal 8-mm diamond-shaped glass bead

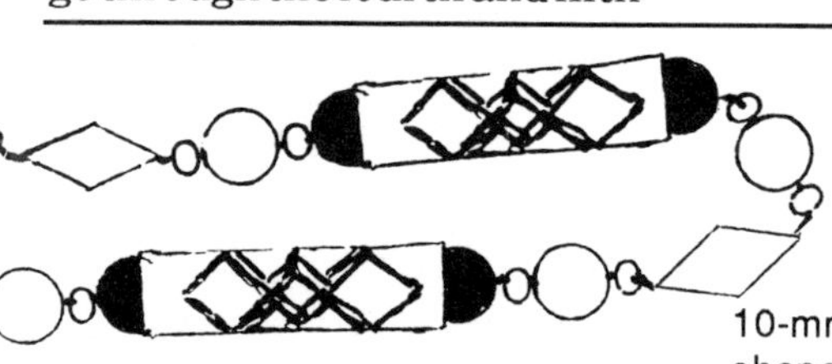

* Foundation row

Dancing Ladies
(Project J)

This project was made using size 11 seed beads and size 5 bugle beads. The foundation row has 6 pairs of seed beeds. To make this pair of earrings, you will need:

- six-inch piece of 3/32-inch brass tubing
- 304 light blue seed beads
- 138 dark blue seed beads
- 136 dusty pink seed beads
- 88 white seed beads
- 88 silver bugle beads
- a pair of ear wires

Make two tubular shapes on a piece of brass tubing 3/32 of an inch in diameter, following the graph. When you have completed the cylinder shape, leave the work on the tubing to add the fringe. You will add fringe to the bottom row of beads added in pairs. Treat this row as you would the foundation row if you were making a pair of flat earrings. Add fringe as indicated in the pattern all the way around the cylinder.

After the fringe is complete, you are ready to complete the top of the earring. Remove the earring from the tubing. Weave the needle and thread back through the cylinder so that you exit through the foundation row through bead #1 in the graph. String eight seed beads on the thread. Bring the needle and thread back through the group of beads marked with #2 of the foundation row. Bring the needle and thread back up through bead #3, add three seed beads, go through the fourth and fifth beads of the loop you made at the top of the earring, add three more seed beads and take the needle and thread back through bead #4. Finish off this thread and the tail as indicated in the instructions under Finishing on page 4.

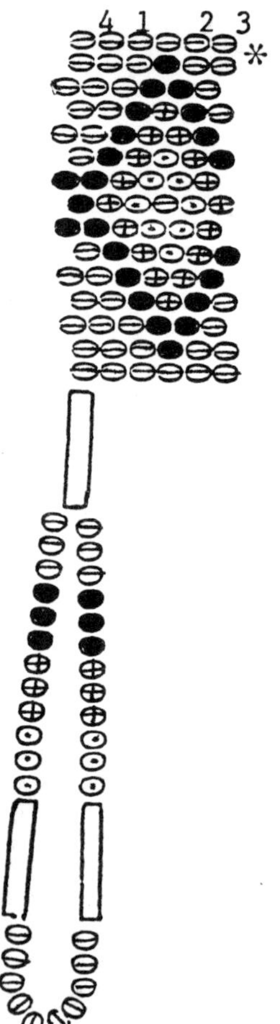

⊖ Light blue
⬤ Dark blue
⊕ Dusty pink
⊙ White

▯ Silver bugle

10-mm diamond shaped bead